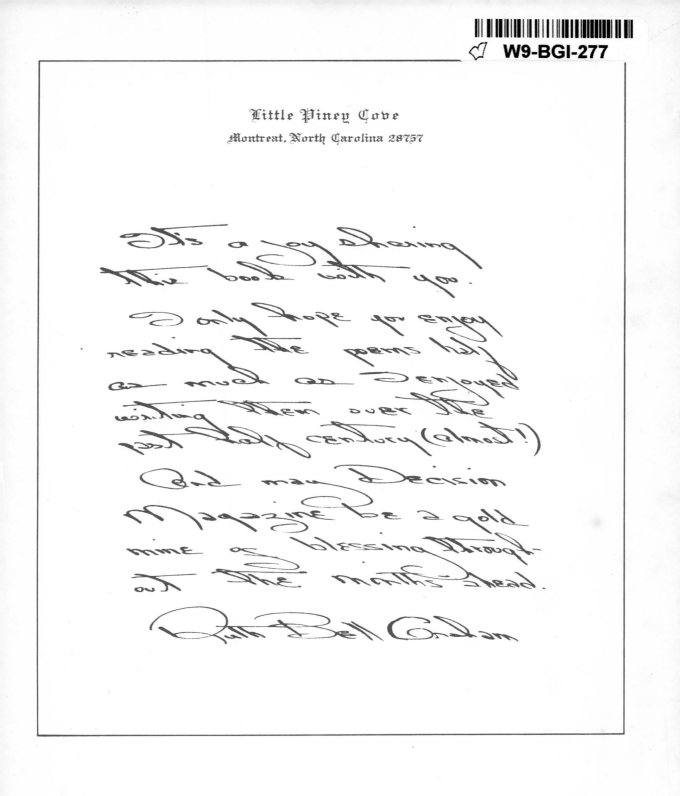

### Little Piney Cove
Montreat, North Carolina 28757

It's a joy sharing
this book with you.

I only hope you enjoy
reading the poems half
as much as I enjoyed
writing them over the
past half century (almost!)

And may Decision
Magazine be a gold
mine of blessing through-
out the months ahead.

Ruth Bell Graham

Sitting by my
laughing fire...

# Sitting by my laughing fire...

## Ruth Bell Graham

Special Edition Published for the
Billy Graham Evangelistic Association

•

**world wide publications**
1303 Hennepin Avenue
Minneapolis, Minnesota 55403

In appreciation

Once, when we were away for some
time, a friend of ours moved into our home
with his wife Anne, his camera, and his
great sensitivity and perception. I handed
him the poems (realizing abstract thoughts
cannot easily be photographed) and said,
"See what you can do." The following
photographs are what he did. With the exception of page 211, all are by Don
Young, and of Little Piney Cove where
we live.

Library of Congress catalog card number: 77-075457
Printed in the United States of America

This special edition is reprinted by
permission of Word Books, Publisher,
Waco, Texas. A deluxe, hardcover, gift
edition is also available.

# By way of explanation

The poems in this book could well be termed the footprints of a pilgrim.

I am, obviously, not a true poet and these poems were never written for publication.

However, I have always loved poetry. As a child in China I used to practice my piano scales while reciting, "Curfew Must Not Ring Tonight." On winter evenings I can remember sitting around the open fire while Daddy (having completed his hospital rounds) read aloud Scott's "The Lady of the Lake," among other classics, while we womenfolk did handwork.

When I went off to what is now North Korea to high school, I was greatly comforted and encouraged by a little volume of Christian verse written by Edith Gilling Cherry of England— a parting gift from our former tutor.

At college in the States I discovered the poems of Amy Carmichael of India, whose prose I had enjoyed while growing up in China. Here I also discovered many of the great classical poets. And in years since then I have come to appreciate a host of other poets, both secular and religious, including the poems of George MacDonald which, while not necessarily great poetry, stretch both mind and heart.

That I could never approach these writers in ability was no deterrent. I wrote because, at times, I had to. It was write, or develop an ulcer—or forget. I chose to write. At times I even wrote for sheer fun.

Although they span nearly half a century of living, beginning with a thirteen-year-old's impression of the ever-present graves in China, through high school in Korea, college in America, early love poems, marriage and motherhood, and on up to now, they are not, by any stretch of the imagination, all autobiographical. Nor, with the exception of pages 14-17, are they arranged chronologically. Nor, for your sake, are they all included.

Many were written concerning people or situations about which I felt deeply. Some know that certain poems were written for or about them. Others do not. But I have chosen not to identify these, preferring that each one who may read them will find in them that which "speaks to their condition." For the same reason explanations, wherever possible, have been avoided.

If they are a mixture—well, that's life.

These are for
YOU

Sitting by my laughing fire...

Sitting by my laughing fire
I watch the whitening world without,
and hear the wind climb higher, higher,
rising to a savage shout;
and on my hearth
the logs smile on,
warming me
as they slowly perish;
they had been felled
by ax and saw
while fellow trees
were left to flourish;
but what was spared
by ax and saw,
by some unspoken,
cruel law,
was being harvested without
by ice and wind
and savage shout.

\* \* \*

And on my hearth
the logs smile on.

Little Piney Cove, 1973

*"China is veritably a country of graves . . ."*
*—from an old book on China*

Look o'er the fields about you—
rivetéd, hilléd with graves;
no one can count the number
of those who perished as slaves;
slaves to the sin they were born in,
knowing not God or His Light;
died without God's great salvation,
died in the darkness of night.

Look o'er the people about you—
faces so furrowed with care,
lined and hardened by sorrow
sin has placed on them there;
think of the evil they live in,
hopes none and joys so few;
love them, pray for them, win them,
lest they should perish, too.

Tsingkiangpu (or Quingqiiang on my latest map of China),
Kiangsu, China, 1933

Lord, when my soul is weary
and my heart is tired and sore,
and I have that failing feeling
that I can't take any more;
then let me know the freshening
found in simple, childlike prayer,
when the kneeling soul knows surely
that a listening Lord is there.

Pyeng Yang (now Pyong Yang, North Korea) 1934

Test me, Lord, and give me strength
to meet each test
   unflinching, unafraid;
not striving nervously to do my best,
not self-assured, or careless as in jest,
   but with Your aid.

Purge me, Lord, and give me grace
to bear the heat
   of cleansing flame;
not bitter at my lowly lot, but meet
to bear my share of suffering and keep sweet,
   in Jesus' Name.

Aboard the S.S. President McKinley, leaving China for college
in America. Fall 1937.

Teach me contentment, Lord, whate'er my lot,
keeping my eyes on You in trust,
knowing Your love is true, Your way is just.

Teach discontentment, Lord, with what I am;
daily striving, growing daily nearer,
finding You are daily closer, dearer.

Contented, Lord, yet discontented make me,
both together working, blending
all in Your own glory ending.

First week at college, 1937

"...to the hills"...

"I will lift up mine eyes
to the hills;"*
and when I fly
I will lift up my eyes
instead
to the sky;
it is the same
sure,
certain thing—
this quiet lifting up,
remembering . . .

I leave myself
awhile
to let my thoughts
explore
all He has made
and More;
returning
to my small load
at length,
calm,
reassured:
this
is my strength.

*Psalm 121:1

17

Abraham,
the friend of God,
with an only son
and a knife at his belt,
". . . Hero of the faith . . ."
Yet I've wondered
at times
how Isaac felt:
his father's hand
stretched forth to kill,
—himself
the sacrificial lamb . . .
It does not say:
yet he grew
to serve
the God of his father
Abraham.

Genesis 22

Lay them quietly at His feet
    one by one:
each desire, however sweet,
    just begun;
dreams still hazy, growing bright;
hope just poised, winged for flight;
all your longing—each delight—
    every one.

At His feet and leave them there,
    never fear;
every heartache, crushing care—
    trembling tear;
you will find Him always true,
men may fail you, friends be few,
He will prove Himself to you
    far more dear.

Dear God,
let me soar in the face of the wind;
up—
up—
like the lark,
so poised and so sure,
through the cold
on the storm
with wings to endure.
Let the silver rain wash
all the dust from my wings,
let me soar
as he soars,
let me sing
as he sings;
let it lift me
all joyous
and carefree
and swift,
let it buffet
and drive me
but, God,
let it lift!

Bless him,
Lord,
in leaving
all
for You—
bereft;
bless him,
Lord,
but pity
the left.

Bless the sacrificial,
yielding
the dearly priced;
bless him,
Lord,
but pity
the sacrificed.

Bless each valiant warrior
wherever he
may roam;
bless him,
Lord,
but pity
those back home.

I met a foreign student once, having a great time with a group
of friends. Someone mentioned how much he had sacrificed
to come here, leaving a wife and six children behind.

Not fears
I need deliverance from
today—
but nothingness;
inertia,
skies gray
and windless;
no sun,
no rain,
no stab of joy
or pain,
no strong regret,
no reaching after,
no tears,
no laughter,
no black despair,
no bliss.
Deliver me
today
. . . from this.

Over on Little Piney Ridge...

Over on Little Piney Ridge,
half a mile from my window sill,
the trees, stripped down
to their winter briefs,
crowded together along the hill
as if for warmth,
and all was still;
when one small,
stubborn,
wrinkled,
leaf,
caught by a stray breeze
passing by,
sprang to life,
waved,
and caught my eye—
Over on Little Piney Ridge.

The future is a blank without a view.
That which I wanted most, You have denied;
I cannot understand (and I have tried);
there's nothing I can do but wait on You.

Earth offered much, and I had, lingering long
outside her lighted windows, wistful grown—
till at my side I heard a voice—Your own.
Lord, how could I resist a love so strong?

Take all away. I am content to know
such love is mine—for life is all too brief
to grieve for pleasures bringing only grief;
give me but You; it is enough just so.

Enough—and more! Such love in You keeps growing—
in You I find my deepest joy complete,
all longing satisfied, and pain made sweet;
in You my cup is filled to overflowing.

The two ways part now and I stand
  uncertain and perplexed.
  Whither, Lord, next?

One friend says this, another that.
  I have no choice.
  Lord, for Thy voice.

But look! one path is stained with blood.
  Footprints I see.
  I follow Thee.

I shall leave it here
beneath this star
tonight;
no one will see me
leave it
with only a star
for light;
no one will know
I stood here,
hoarding a heaviness,
clutching tightly
in eager hands
something of loveliness;
something
that struggled against me
striving for liberty:
I'll love it,
and leave it,
and then forget;
and forgetting—
I shall be free!

Dear God, I prayed, all unafraid
(as we're inclined to do)
I do not need a handsome man
but let him be like You;
I do not need one big and strong
nor yet so very tall,
nor need he be some genius,
or wealthy, Lord, at all;
but let his head be high, dear God,
and let his eye be clear,
his shoulders straight, whate'er his state,
whate'er his earthly sphere;
and let his face have character,
a ruggedness of soul,
and let his whole life show, dear God,
a singleness of goal;
then when he comes
(as he will come)
with quiet eyes aglow,
I'll understand that he's the man
I prayed for long ago.

Winter speaks
to the surfeited heart,
weary of heat
and weeds
and leaves,
longing to breathe
cold, bracing air,
explore the hillsides
swept and bare;
to revel in
each bush,
each tree
stripped to stark
simplicity;
original etchings
everywhere—

and You,
Who etched them,
with me there.

I awoke heavy...

I awoke heavy
and heavy I prayed,
face in the sun,
heart in the shade.
As smoke hangs low
on a sullen day,
my prayer hung there . . .
till I heard His voice,
"This is the day
that the Lord hath made;
. . . Rejoice . . . !"*

We Peters
walking on life's sea,
implore ignoring grace
of heaving waves;*
oh, let us be,
however weak,
intent on Thee;
our eyes upon Thy face.

*Psalm 118:24

*Matthew 14:30

I looked into your face and knew
that you were true;
those clear, deep eyes awoke in me
a trust in you.

I'd dreamt of shoulders broad and straight,
one built to lead;
I met you once and knew that you
were all I need.

You did not have to say a word
to make me feel
that will, completely in control,
was made of steel.

I'd dreamt of dashing love and bold,
life wild with zest;
but when with you my heart was stilled
to perfect rest.

And how? I could not understand,
it seemed so odd:
till on my heart it quietly dawned
—love is of God!

In the weary,
waiting,
silence
of the night,
speak to me, Lord!
The others do—
haunting,
accusing,
foreboding;
the body tosses
and
the heart grows tight,
and
sleep, elusive, fades into
the
weary,
waiting,
silence
of the night.

He speaks:
the mind,
preoccupied with sleeplessness,
is deaf.
Silently
He wraps me in His love;
so loved,
I rest.

They felt good eyes upon them
and shrank within—undone;
good parents had good children
and they—a wandering one.

The good folk never meant
to act smug or condemn,
but having prodigals
just "wasn't done" with them.

Remind them gently, Lord,
how You
have trouble with Your children,
too.

Let it be twilight

Let it be twilight
just a little longer . . .
don't turn the lights up
yet;
twilight's a time
for remembering,
twilight's a time
to forget;
a decompression chamber
where the soul
submerged, uptight,
can un-begin
and slowly rise
to night.

My love has long been yours . . .
since on that day
when we first met;
I will never quite forget
how you just paused
and smiled a bit,
then calmly helped yourself to it.

"He took . . .
and blessed
and broke . . .''*
the Scriptures say,
the bread
with which those hungry folk
were fed
that day.

\* \* \*

And by this simple act
—so oddly His—
two, bewildered
by their loss
(whose Life had died
upon a cross,
pierced by nail and sword);
those two, eyes opened,
saw in this
their Risen Lord.‡

\* \* \*

Lord,
when I dread
to be
broken bread
and poured out wine
for You,
to satisfy man's hunger,
quench man's thirst,
remind me
how You blessed it
first.

*Matthew 14:19    ‡Luke 24:30

Never turn your back
on tears,
do not stem the flow;
put your arms about her
gently,
let her go.

Knowing why
is not important,
weeping
sometimes is.
Let her cry
—but kindly—
with a kiss.

Your eyes
look down at me
so thoughtfully . . .
What do they see?
The plainness of me—
plainly built,
not small,
nor calmly poised,
nor quaint,
and, worst of all,
a nose upturned
and hands
that I have known
for years to be
too long, too overgrown;
plain hazel eyes,
a face too pale,
not fair,
a mouth too large
and ordinary hair?

And all of me
tucked in
this homemade dress;
oh, if you look at me
so thoughtfully,
will you love me
the less?

Bravely the little bird clung there
   out in the storm;
torn by each blast that was flung there,
chirped to keep himself warm;
ruffled his feathers and clung there,
till frozen and stiff it hung there,
spring came and still it swung there,
   all that was left of the storm.

I found it caught by a string.

...Truth here revealed...

"This is My body
broken like bread for you;
this is My blood
like water shed for you."*
Drink it—and wonder.
Marvel—and eat.
God torn asunder,
man made complete!
Stagger the mind
at Truth here revealed:
kneel—and be broken,
rise—and be healed.
Go out and die,
die 'live, and live!
Take all He offers,
take all and give.
Here's a remembering
to scorch and to bless:
sinners partaking
God's righteousness.

* * *

Lord,
this is my body . . .

*Luke 22:19, 20

God,
let me be all he ever dreamed
of loveliness and laughter.
Veil his eyes a bit
because
there are so many little flaws;
somehow, God,
please let him see
only the bride I long to be,
remembering ever after—
I was all he ever dreamed
of loveliness and laughter.

Perhaps
she will land
upon That Shore,
not in full sail,
but rather,
a bit of broken wreckage
for Him
to gather.

Perhaps
He walks Those Shores
seeking such,
who have believed
a little,
suffered much
and so,
been washed Ashore.

Perhaps
of all the souls redeemed
they most
adore.

Pray
when all your soul
a tiptoe stands
in wistful eagerness
to talk with God;
put out your hands,
God bends to hear;
it would be sin
not to draw near.

Pray
when gray inertia
creeps through your soul,
as through a man
who fights the cold,
then growing languid
slumbereth,
and slumbering
knows not
it is death.

Pray
when swamped
with sin and shame
and nowhere else
to pin the blame
but your own will
and waywardness;
God knows you,
loves you nonetheless.

So . . .
pray.

"With this ring . . ."
your strong, familiar voice
fell like a benediction
on my heart, that dusk;
tall candles flickered gently,
our age-old vows were said,
and I could hear
someone begin to sing
an old, old song,
timeworn and lovely,
timeworn and dear.
And in that dusk
were old, old friends—
and you,
an old friend, too,
(and dearer than them all).
Only my ring seemed new—
its plain gold
surface
warm and bright
and strange to me
that candlelight . . .
unworn—unmarred.
Could it be that wedding rings
like other things,
are lovelier when scarred?

"And when Messiah comes,"
he said,
(his eyes looked through me
and beyond,
the food forgotten
on his plate,
silent
he let the minutes wait
as light dawned).
"And when Messiah comes,"
he said,
the strange thought
gripped him—
strong, sublime,
repelled and beckoned—
"I shall ask—
'Is this the first time
. . . or the second?'"

The candle flames of poplars...

The candle flames
of poplars,
in the little coves
burn low;
The woods, leaf-carpeted
are warm
with Autumn's afterglow.
There's frost
upon the air tonight,
a hint of coming cold;
still, the warmth
of summer lingers
in the crimson
and the gold.

Give me a cove
—a little cove—
when Fall comes
amblin' round:
hint of frost
upon the air,
sunlight
on the ground;
a little cove
with poplars—
calm
and
straight
and
tall;
to burn like candle flames
against
the sullen gray
of Fall.

Little Piney Cove

The load
that lay
like lead
lifted;
instead:
peace.

The dread
that hung
fog-thick, gray,
faded away;
and with release,
day.

The trial
the same . . .
unsolved,
but this:
now
it is
His.

I walked today
through loud, crisp leaves;
back to the sun,
face to the breeze;
and where I sat
to enjoy the view,
a grasshopper sat
enjoying it, too:
("of sober color,"
except for thighs,
protectively striped,
which did seem wise).
And there in the warm sun,
side by side,
each viewed the view
and each one eyed
the other. Odd, we two:
below us lay
the valley floor
which Fall, with blue haze,
failed to smother;
splendor unmatched
on which to gaze—
and each
distracted by the other!

Little Piney Cove

For all
who knew the shelter of The Fold,
its warmth and safety
and The Shepherd's care,
and bolted;
choosing instead to fare
out into the cold,
the night;
revolted
by guardianship,
by Light;
lured
by the unknown;
eager to be out
and on their own;
freed
to water where they may,
feed
where they can,
live as they will:
till
they are cured,
let them be cold,
ill;
let them know terror,

feed
them with thistle,
weed,
and thorn;
who chose
the company of wolves,
let them taste
the companionship wolves give
to helpless strays;
but, oh! let them live—
wiser, though torn!
And wherever,
however far away
they roam,
follow
and
watch
and
keep
Your stupid, wayward, stubborn sheep,
and someday
bring them Home!

There will be less someday—
much less,
and there will be More:
less to distract
and amuse;
More, to adore;
less to burden
and confuse;
More, to undo
the cluttering of centuries,
that we might view
again, That which star
and angels
pointed to;
we shall be poorer—
and richer;
stripped—and free:
for always there will be a Gift,
always
a Tree!

Christmas reverie

His presence and His Word..

Plenty
is always provision for a need:
another's
or some future of our own—
unrealized, perhaps;
unseen.
The seven years of plenty*
Joseph stored
against the years of famine
that would come.
So
when a winter
promises to be
severe,
nature generously provides
for little friends;
and sensing
in her lavish spread
a hint of coming want,
the ants
and squirrels are busy
harvesting;
and so am I.
I have been
so generously provided for
in happiness,
good memories,
family,
and true friends;
and more than all—

His presence and His Word;
perhaps it is a "sign,"
as mountain people say,
that winter is to be
a tough one.
If that is so,
let it be;
my larders are well stocked.

*Genesis 41

Never let it end, God,
never—please—
all this growing loveliness,
all of these
brief moments of
fresh pleasure—
never let it end.
Let us always
be a little
breathless at love's beauty;
never let us
pause to reason
from a sense of duty;
never let us
stop to measure
just how much to give;
never let us
stoop to weigh love;
let us live—
and live!
Please, God,
let our hearts kneel always,
Love their only master,
knowing the warm impulsiveness
of shattered alabaster:*
I know You can see things
the way a new bride sees,
so
never let it end, God,
never—please.


Hinsdale, Illinois, Fall 1943
*Mark 14:3

"I am thy shield,
and thy
exceeding great reward,"*
Could heart wish more
than this,
O Lord,
my Lord?

*Genesis 15:1

O Thou,
Whose stillness drowns
earth's total noise—
its grating sounds:
progress,
traffic,
voice;
flutterings
of my frustration,
mutterings,
agitation;
the screaming silences
without,
within;
the din
of questions clamoring
for their "why?"
and "how?"
now!
the rumblings
of man's discontent,
erupting hate,
violence;
war's distant thunder
rolling near,
and everywhere
the cries
of fear
that paralyzes
as it grips . . .

and near at hand
a faucet drips.

O Thou,
Whose stillness drowns
earth's total noise,
only in Thee
is stillness found . . .
And I
rejoice.

Tell me
how
the setting sun,
briefly glimpsed
through wet
black clouds,
can
to molten gold
with ease,
kindle
sodden limbs
of trees.

I lay my "whys"
before Your Cross
in worship kneeling,
my mind too numb
for thought,
my heart beyond
all feeling.

And worshiping,
realize that I
in knowing You
don't need a "why."

Odd this twisted form...

Odd
this twisted form
should be
the work of
God.
God
Who makes,
without mistakes,
the happy norm,
the status quo,
the usual,
made me,
you know.
The Royal Palm
He made;
and, too,
the stunted pine.
With joy
I see the lovely shapes.
With pride
I live in mine.

* * *

No accident I am:
a Master Craftsman's plan.

The field that night
was a sea of mud,
the wet sky
seared with flame;
each bursting shell,
like a blast from hell,
lit the spot
where a soldier fell.

There in the blackness,
lying low,
weakly
he spoke His Name.

For
where the lust of man
runs loose
through stench and smoke
of hate white-hot,
where lives
and souls
are cheaply priced,
there walks the Christ.

The sin-scarred
brush
His white, white robes;
the wounded
touch
His feet;
the dying
whisper
His name in prayer,

wondering sweetly
to find Him
there,
where hell
and the sinner
meet.

* * *

He took of His grace:
His infinite grace—

And soldiers wondered
to find a trace
of tears
in the grime
on a dead man's face.
''The going
must've been tough,''
they said,
not knowing,
that death,
for a man
forgiven by God,
is easy going.

An owl hooted mournfully
this noon:
incongruous, if you please,
as Jeremiah
prophesying doom
in midst of peace.

He is not eloquent,
as men count such;
for him
words trip and stumble
giving speech
an awkward touch,
and humble:
so, much
is left unsaid
that he would say
if he were eloquent.
Wisely discontent,
compassion driven
(as avarice drives some,
ambition others),
the old,
the lonely,
and the outcast come;
all are welcome,
all find a home,
all—his brothers.

Behind him
deeds rise quietly
to stay;
and those with eyes to see
can see
all he can say.

Perhaps he'd not have spent
his life this way
if he were eloquent.

London, 1972

74

That was the Day Between
the Night Before—

The blood
still wet upon the hill;
His body
wrapped,
entombed,
and still;
the great stone sealed
with Roman seal
and guarded well.

Many a Judean home
had now become
a lesser tomb
within whose walls
men lay,
whose Life had died
That Day.

Looking back
we cannot share
their black
despair.
For us
He is the Risen Christ,
as He had said:
for them, that Shabbat,
all life died—
for He was dead.

\* \* \*

That was the Day Between
the Night Before.

\* \* \*

This is my Day Between,
my Night Before . . .

Suspended
in this interim—
let me be still,
let me adore,
let me remember
Him.

Saturday between Good Friday and Easter

75

I leave him in Your hands, O God,
Who are both merciful and just . . .
dumb with the horror of this deed,
its hideous stench, one surely must
know how to pray;
yet I am still—
sickened to silence.
What can one say?
Was he Your son?
If so
then You will know
what must be done:
for he will be in black despair
lest he has sinned
beyond all mercy . . .
all repair.
What he has done,
is done. No prayer . . .
no penance . . . nothing . . .
can undo the loathsome deed.
Yet he
*is* Yours:
and I would plead,
Lord, let him see
long and stark and clear,
Your Calvary.

...my shelf of peace...

This is my ledge
of quiet,
my shelf of peace,
edged
by its crooked rails
holding back the beyond.
Above,
a hawk sails
high
to challenge clouds
trespassing
my plot of sky.
Below
in the valley,
remote and dim,
sounds
come and go,
a requiem
for quiet.
Here on my ledge,
quiet praise:
of birds,
crickets,
breeze—
in different ways;
and so do I—
for these:
my ledge of quiet,
my plot of sky:
for peace.

Little Piney Cove

As the portrait is unconscious
of the master artist's touch,
unaware of growing beauty,
unaware of changing much,
so you have not guessed His working
in your life throughout each year,
have not seen the growing beauty
have not sensed it, Mother dear.
We have seen and marveled greatly
at the Master Artist's skill,
marveled at the lovely picture
daily growing lovelier still;
watched His brush strokes
change each feature
to a likeness of His face,
till in you we see the Master,
feel His presence, glimpse His grace;
pray the fragrance of His presence
may through you seem doubly sweet,
till your years on earth are ended
and the portrait is complete.

Mother's Day, 1940
Portrait completed, November 8, 1974

It seems irreverent to fly
above
snow-capped peaks;
mountains tall enough
to earn the snows,
deserve respect;
they were made
to be looked up to,
not down upon,
by man.

* * *

Fly humbly,
when you fly;
walk,
when you can.

Love
without clinging;
cry
if you must—
but privately cry;
the heart will adjust
to the newness of loving
in practical ways:
cleaning
and cooking
and sorting out clothes,
all say, "I love you,"
when lovingly done.

So—
love
without clinging;
cry—
if you must—
but privately cry;
the heart will adjust
to the length of his stride,
the song he is singing,
the trail he must ride,
the tensions that make him
the man that he is,
the world he must face,
the life that is his.

So
love
without clinging;
cry—
if you must—
but privately cry;
the heart will adjust
to being the heart,
not the forefront of life;
a part of himself,
not the object—
his wife.

So—
love!

I knew a Malchus once.
Severely wounded
by a Peter's sword:
crazed by anger;
dazed by pain,
he thrust aside
with awful pride
that Gentle Hand
Whose touch alone
could make him
whole again.
"Have Jesus touch me?
Hell!" he hissed,
"'twas His disciple
swung the sword,
aiming for my neck
and missed;
I want no part
of Peter's Lord!"

Strong Savior Christ
so oft repelled,
for rash disciples
blamed!

Poor wounded fools,
by pride compelled
to go on living
—maimed!

John 18

Where I hid my little nest...

All my leaves have fallen,
and all the world can see
where I hid my little nest
safe, within this tree.

All my leaves have fallen,
and yet, another year,
when I have need to hide my nest,
the leaves will reappear.

Five I have:
each separate,
distinct,
a soul
bound for eternity:
and I
—blind
leader of the blind—
groping and fumbling,
casual and concerned,
by turns . . .
undisciplined, I seek
by order and command
to discipline and shape;
(I who need
Thy discipline
to shape
my own disordered soul).
O Thou
Who seest the heart's
true, deep desire,
each shortcoming and
each sad mistake,
supplement
and
overrule,
nor let our children be
the victims of our own
unlikeness unto Thee.

Samson—
man of giant strength—
pillowed his great head upon
the lap of sin
then rose at length
"not knowing
that his strength was gone."

Judges 16:20

You look at me
and see
my flaws;
I look at you
and see
flaws, too.
Those who love,
know love
deserves
a second glance;
each failure serves
another chance.
Love looks to see,
beyond the scars
and flaws,
the cause;
and scars become
an honorable badge
of battles fought
and won—
(or lost)
but fought!
The product,
not the cost,
is what love sought.

\* \* \*

God help us see
beyond the now
to the before,
and note with tenderness
what lies between
—and love the more!

When my Fall comes
I wonder—
will I feel
as I feel now,
glutted with happy memories,
content
to let them lie
like nuts
stored up against the coming cold?
Squirrels always gather—
so I'm told—
more than they will ever need;
and so have I.

Will the dry,
bitter smell of Fall,
the glory of the
dying leaves,
the last brave rose
against the wall
fill me with quiet ecstasy
as they do now?

Will my thoughts turn
without regret,
from blackened borders,
leafless trees,
to the warm comforts
that a winter brings
—of hearth fires,
   books
  and inner things—
and find them nicer yet?

I climbed the hills
through yesterday:
and I am young
and strong again;
my children climb
these hills with me,
and all the time
they shout and play;
their laughter fills
the coves among
the rhododendron and the oak
till we have struggled to
the ridge top
where the chestnuts grew.
Breathless, tired, and content
we let the mountain
breeze blow through
our busy minds
and through our hair
refresh our bodies hot and spent
and drink
from some cool mountain spring,
the view refreshing everything—
Infinity, with hills between,
silent, hazy, wild-serene.
Then . . .
when I return to now
I pray,
"Thank You, God,
for yesterday."

The hills on which I need to gaze...

The hills on which I need to gaze
are wrapped in clouds again.
I lift up streaming eyes in vain
and feel upon my upturned face
the streaming rain.

Those seals—
weight of empires,
authority of kings;
dread power
compressed to make
it worth one's life
to break
those seals;

no mortal dared;
no matter when,
no matter whom.

One secured
a lion's den;*
one
a borrowed tomb.‡

Lausanne, Switzerland

*Daniel 6:17
‡Matthew 27:66

For all these smallnesses
I thank You, Lord:

small children
and small needs;
small meals to cook,
small talk to heed,
and a small book
from which to read
small stories;
small hurts to heal,
small disappointments, too,
as real
as ours;
small glories
to discover
in bugs,
pebbles,
flowers.

When day is through
my mind is small,
my strength is gone;
and as I gather
each dear one
I pray, "Bless each
for Jesus' sake—
such angels sleeping,
imps awake!"

What wears me out
are little things:
angels minus
shining wings.
Forgive me, Lord,
if I have whined;
. . . it takes so much
to keep them shined;
yet each small rub
has its reward,
for they have blessed *me*.

Thank You,
Lord.

Is the tree that's pruned
preoccupied with pain?
—standing with its wound
in the wind and rain;
shrouded in cool mist,
kissed by the dew,
chosen for a nest
by a bird or two;
enveloped by fragrance
of rainwashed air,
bloodroots and violets
clustered round it there;
gently transfigured
as sap begins to flow—
leaves, flowers,
choicest fruit—
how I'd like to know:
Is the tree that's pruned
preoccupied with pain?

What of the folk back home
that day
the sudden storm swept Galilee?*
Knowing the violence of those storms,
the smallness of the craft,
did they
abandon themselves to grief,
or say,
"The One who sails with them
is He
Who made the storm-filled universe,
the height,
the depth,
the everywhere;
the storm is fierce,
the craft is small,
but
He is there!"?

*Mark 4:37

98

... then let it snow ...

If I could have each day
one hour of sun,
       glorious,
       healing,
       hot,
like now—
then
let Winter come!
Not
mild and brief,
but
wild, without relief;
let the storms rage,
let the winds blow,
the freezing rains
lashing my windowpanes;
then
let it snow!
long
and
deep
and cold.

I would not mind at all:
it would be fun . . .
if I could have
each day
my hour of sun.

God,
what a waste!

He was so needed
by us all
. . . by You.
and yet You kill,
it seems at will,
Your young,
Your trained,
Your highly skilled
(and not a few)—
Stephen first
. . . then James . . .
and . . .
O God!
our Savior, too.

Did I say
"waste"?
Forgive
the stupid words
we cry
in anguished haste.

The Gardener
plants
and reaps
with skill.

. . . it's only
that we're left here
still.

It seems but yesterday
you lay
new in my arms.
Into our lives you brought
sunshine
and laughter—
play—
showers, too,
and song.
Headstrong,
heartstrong,
gay,
tender beyond believing,
simple in faith,
clear-eyed,
shy,
eager for life—
you left us
rich in memories,
little wife.
And now today
I hear you say
words wise beyond your years;
I watch you play
with your small son,
tenderest of mothers.
Years slip away—

today
we are mothers
together.

Gstaad, Switzerland

This is a gentle part of town
—run down.
Papers blow about the street,
people walk on tired feet,
discount stores, a place to eat,
hardware, garden stuff and such:
shabby. No, there isn't much
to see. And yet,
here's a part I can't forget.
It isn't something
I just feel:
but folks are folks here,
folks are real,
folks are simple,
folks are kind,
if you don't buy much
they don't mind.
It's just a gentle part of town
—run down.

Die, son:
but do not sin.
It is too high a price
for living—
if "life" it can be called
to wallow
(briefly even)
in that which God forbids.
Satan has desired you:
shrewd,
he will not use
revolting sins
to lure,
but "lovely" ones,
"respectable,"
"desirable,"
and "pure"
(or so they seem);
far better you should die
honorably,
and clean
than craven-hearted,
nearsighted,
weak of will
and mean,
your birthright you should sell
for a mere mess of pottage,[1]
squander your inheritance
in wild living,
then fain
fill your belly with
the husks of swine.[2]

Would you trade
fellowship with Him
for tarnished coin
and raveled end of rope?[3]

God's hand is on you, son;
far better then
the furnace, seven-times heated,[4]
the denned and starving lions,[5]
the stones that honored Stephen,[6]
or a cross . . .

The choice is yours:
God grant you
eyes to see
and ears to hear,
a loyal heart
and will of steel,
forged to His will,
sound in His fear.

So . . .
die;
but do not sin;

such death
is not life's end—
but its beginning.[7]

1. Genesis 25
2. Luke 15
3. Matthew 27:5
4. Daniel 3:19
5. Daniel 6:16
6. Acts 7:59
7. Matthew 10:39

The growing darkness closes in...

*"When I said, darkness will surely trample me down,
then to my great joy, night was luminous."*
                                    Psalm 138:11, LXX

*"The Lord said that He would dwell in the thick
darkness."*
                                    1 Kings 8:12

The growing darkness closes in
like some thick fog,
engulfing me—
a creeping horror—
till I learned,
"the darkness hideth not from Thee."*

        * * *

"The earth was without form
and void."
Upon the deep
such darkness lay:
O Light, Who first created light,‡
do Thou the same
today!

        * * *

As in a darkened room
one knows—
knows without sight—
another there,
so, in the darkness,
sure I knew
Thy presence,

and the cold despair,
formless and chaotic, merged
to a soft glory;
as a child
terrified by dark,
lies quiet
within his mother's arms,
no wild
fears shall torment,
my weakness now.
The dark—the dark—
surrounds me still.
But so dost Thou!

*Psalm 139:12
‡Genesis 1:2-3

109

An ancient oak
among the trees
stood in the freezing
winter air;
lifeless it was
and stripped of leaves—
only a few dead leaves
hung there.
I watched all winter—
watched to see
how long
those shriveled leaves
would cling,
like withered hands,
upon the tree
where whipping winds
would bite and sting.
Each day I watched
and watched in vain;
snowstorms came
and blizzards blew,
wind, ice and sleet,
hailstorms and rain:
each took its turn.
When all was through,
those leaves
were still there
clinging fast:
then—
came Spring.
Life throbbed anew
within the tree
and loosed their clasp.

He hung his heart
on a fence for sale,
then sat in his van
and watched them pass:
some, just out for a Sunday stroll,
glancing at the art en masse;
others, curious; and a few,
souvenir hunting
(as tourists do)
paused to price as well as stare:
—and part of himself
hung drying there:
years of feeling,
hours of toil—
(acrylic was faster;
he chose oil).
So when some tourist asked,
"How much?"
He'd smile and say,
"It's wet. Don't touch."

He needed to sell his work
and yet . . .

Bayswater Road, London

Carefree, she stepped into the sunlight,
her face uplifted to the sun;
while I,
aware of brewing storms
that etched
the sky,
clutched at a fear
and nursed it.
Then I
saw her hand
outstretched
like a small child;
and while
I watched,
Another Hand
reached down and clasped it.

I heard the distant thunder
with a smile.

London

Death—
death can be faced,
dealt with,
adjusted to,
outlived.
It's the
not knowing,
that destroys
interminably . . .
This
being suspended
in suspense;
waiting—weightless.
How does one face
the faceless,
adjust to nothing?
Waiting implies
something to wait for.
Is there?

There is One.
One Who knows
where he is
and if;
and if he is,
is with him;
and if not,
is with me.
God, Thou art!
I rest my soul on that.

I rest
him,
my hopes,
my fears,
my all—
on That.
Someday
I shall know,
and knowing
worship.
So—
today
I worship, too.

October 8, 1971
For the wives and families of those
Missing in Action.

May he face life's problems
as he faced
his broken bike
when he was small,
working till he'd traced
each problem to its source,
and fixed it; all
was a challenge he'd accept
with curiosity and then
work night and day.
What's losing sleep when
interest is involved?
Hobby or problem
he never turned it loose
till it was solved.

Now
he's a man.
And man-sized problems
stare him in the face.
Interested or not,
Lord,
give him grace.
As this is a problem tough,
and not a toy,
so, too, he is a man now
Lord
—not a boy.

(Yet in the boy he once was
I could see
delightful glimpses of the man
that he would be.)

The closing of a door

We live a time
secure;
beloved and loving,
sure
it cannot last
for long
then—
the goodbyes come
again—again—
like a small death,
the closing of a door.
One learns to live
with pain.
One looks ahead,
not back—
never back,
only before.
And joy will come again—
warm and secure,
if only for the now,
laughing,
we endure.

Had I been Joseph's mother
I'd have prayed
protection from his brothers:
"God keep him safe;
he is so young,
so different from
the others."
Mercifully
she never knew
there would be slavery
and prison, too.*

Had I been Moses' mother
I'd have wept
to keep my little son;
praying she might forget
the babe drawn from the water
of the Nile,
had I not kept
him for her
nursing him the while?
Was he not mine
and she
but Pharaoh's daughter?‡

Had I been Daniel's mother
I should have pled
"Give victory!
This Babylonian horde—
godless and cruel—
don't let them take him captive
—better dead,
Almighty Lord!"**

Had I been Mary—
Oh, had I been she,
I would have cried
as never mother cried,
". . . Anything, O God,
anything . . .
but crucified!"

With such prayers
importunate
my finite wisdom
would assail
Infinite Wisdom;

God, how fortunate
Infinite Wisdom
should prevail!

*Genesis 37
‡Exodus 2
**Daniel 1

Why
argue,
and fight,
and worry
how the world ends?
Pray for the best,
prepare for the worst,
and take whatever God sends.

The little things that bug me,
resentments deep within;
the things I ought to do, undone,
the irritations one by one
till nerves stretch screaming-thin
and bare for all the world to see—
which needs His touch to make it whole
the most, my body or my soul?

I pray—but nothing comes out right,
my thoughts go flying everywhere;
my attitudes are all confused,
I hate myself—I am not used
to hands all clenched, not clasped, in prayer,
and heart too leaden to take flight;
which, oh, which, needs to be whole
the most, my body or my soul?

I cannot read. I cannot pray.
I cannot even think.
Where to from here? and how get there
with only darkness everywhere?
I ought to rise and only sink . . .
and feel His arms, and hear Him say,
"I love you." . . . It was all my soul
or body needed to be whole.

There are no depths
to which I have gone
or to which I could go,
but Thou, in Thy fathomless
mercy and love
didst still sink below,
plumbing the depths
for a sin-ruined heart
indifferent to Thee;
draining the dregs
of God's holy wrath
that I might go free.

Each man has his Isaac
(each lesser Abraham);
some "only son"
God says must die:
and so have I.

Yet all the time I wonder,
what if there is no ram?
No staying hand,
no quick reprieve,
to let mine live?

Genesis 22

Beauty distilled by solitude...

Beauty distilled
by solitude,
unrivaled by
the burnt-out wood;
glory unfurled
against a world
stripped and chilled—
by death subdued;
such lonely,
gay defiance speaks
more than Fall's prime
could,
more than Fall's peak.

Theirs
is a still-less,
restless grave—
dismantled
by each churning wave,
each tugging tide,
and pried
by treasure seekers, till
they know no rest
—who should be still.

One offered me
old coin for new;
priced as high
as they were few;
I held them in my hands
with awe—
two hundred years
I touched and saw,
but thought,
treasure should be found—
not bought.

And so, I searched:
training my eyes
to spot time's clever,
sure disguise.
My mind wheeled freely
with the gulls,
watching for cannon,
rusting hulls,
probing for treasure
(beneath that vast

impersonal guardian
of the past—
slapping indifferently
the beach),
buried,
barnacled,
out of reach.

A wistful beggar
asked an alm
from that
vast,
wet,
unyielding palm.

Then . . .

I thought of old,
wrecked lives
yielding
their treasure store
with each new storm;
and I had found,
not what I sought,
but more.

Vero Beach, Florida

Spanish galleons sank in a storm off the coast between Ft.
Pierce and Sebastian Inlet in the 1700s.

"And do storms always stir up the treasure that's there?" I
asked someone who knows about such things.

"Not always," he replied. "Sometimes it buries it deeper.
Depending on the tides. But there's a lot of treasure out there
still."

The day is long
and all that I must do
too much for my small strength.
When at length
the day is through,
shall I find
I failed to tap
the Infinite Resources
forever open to the weak
who seek?
Shall I die
regretting
not getting?
Shall Joy
weep
for my sake
—who would not
take?

It is this stillness
that I find oppressive:
after the wind
that blew across these hills,
howling around the house—
violent and possessive,
prowling the sills,
slamming the shutters
(if it found one loose),
dying to threatening mutters
and rising to shake
the ancient oak,
hoping some branch
would break—
and when it broke,
chasing the hapless leaves
into whatever corner
they could find
shelter in;
"Oh be kind!"
I'd think, watching it whip and tear
smoke from the chimney
like a thing alive,
whirling it to the ground;
then drive
the clouds as if they were a flock
of frightened sheep.

How long it blew—
a lifetime or a day—
I never knew;
it went away
somewhere near five o'clock,
leaving earth still and thinned:

and I could weep—
who had grown used
to wind.

May she have daughters
of her own
to care
when she is old
and I am gone.
I should have loved
to care for her once more
as I did then
long years before.
I was a mother young
and she—my child.
Caring was joy. So when
she is old and I am There,
may she have daughters
of her own
to care.

Don't talk to me yet;
the wound is fresh,
the nauseous pain
I can't forget
fades into numbness
like a wave,
then comes again.
Your tears I understand,
but grief is deaf;
it cannot hear the words
you gently planned
and tried to say.
But . . .
pray.

I cannot look You in the face, God...

I cannot look You in the face,
God—
these eyes—
bloodshot,
bleary,
blurred;
shoulders slumped,
soul slumped,
heart too blank to care;
fears
worn out by fearing,
life
worn bare by living;
—living?
too old to live,
too young to die.
Who am I?
God—
Why?

"Leave it all quietly to God
my soul":*
the past mistakes
that left
their scars.
All bitterness
beyond control,
that mars
His peace,
demands its toll.
Confessed to Him
. . . and left . . .
it would,
like all things
work together
for my good,
and bring release.
I would be whole.
So
"Leave it all quietly to God
my soul."

*Psalm 62:1, 5 (Moffatt)

134

Of this historic moment
two things I kept:
that earth was gray
and cold,
and heaven wept.

Austin, Texas, January 25, 1973

She waited for the call
that never came;
searched every mail
for a letter,
or a note,
or card,
that bore his name;
and on her knees
at night,
and on her feet
all day,
she stormed Heaven's Gate
in his behalf;
she pled for him
in Heaven's high court.
"Be still, and wait,"
the word He gave;
and so she knew
He would
do in, and for,
and with him,
that which she never could.
Doubts ignored,
she went about her chores
with joy;
knowing, though spurned,
His word was true.
The prodigal had not returned
but God was God,
and there was work to do.

I captured him in Kleenex
and threw him out with care—
the happy little cricket
enlivening the air.
For it was late and I,
tired from the noise of day,
tossed sleepless, then decided my
rest precluded his play.
And so he was moved
without notice: I didn't even wince;
But slept serenely all night long,
. . . and have missed him
ever since.

When death comes
will it come quietly
—one might say creep—
as after a hard
and tiring day, one lies
and longs for sleep—
ending age and sorrow
or youth and pain?
Who dies in Christ
has all to gain
—and a Tomorrow!
Why weep?

Death may be savage.
We cannot be sure:
the godly may be slaughtered,
evil men endure;
however death may strike,
or whom,
who knows the risen Lord
knows, too, the empty tomb.

It won't be long...

It won't be long—
the sun is slowly slipping out of sight;
lengthening shadows deepen into dusk;
still winds whisper;
all is quiet:
it won't be long
—till night.

It won't be long—
the tired eyes close,
her strength is nearly gone;
frail hands that ministered to many
lie quiet, still;
Light from another world!
Look up, bereaved!
It won't be long
—till Dawn!

When a young boy cries
in bed at night,
stealthily,
silently,
never aloud,
newly away
from family and friends,
too old to cry,
too proud;
too young to know
each night passes on
making way
for a newer dawn;
too old
to stay
in the nest, and yet
too young
to fly
away.

God,
be near
when a young boy cries.

*"The gates of Hell are locked from the inside."*
                                          *C. S. Lewis*

If that is so,
he seemed already there;
his guarded eyes
looked out at me
as if through bars;
my words fell unheard
on the stale air,
my heart reached out
and touched a closing door,
the widening gulf between
already wide.
"I pray for you,"
I said and said no more.
The vacant eyes withdrew.

Was the key turning
on the other side?

Those were no ordinary sheep,*      How right
no common flocks,      the angels should appear
huddled in sleep      to them
among the fields,      That Night.
the layered rocks,
near Bethlehem
That Night;
but those
selected for the Temple sacrifice:
theirs to atone
for sins
they had not done.

         * * *

How right
the angels should appear
to them
That Night.

         * * *

Those were no usual shepherds
there,
but outcast shepherds
whose unusual care
of special sheep
made it impossible to keep
Rabbinic law,
which therefore banned them.

*Luke 2 (see Alfred Edersheim, *Jesus the Messiah*) .

He handed it to me
then stood
shyly;
his face,
alight with pride,
searched mine to see
if I'd
be pleased or
if I would
note the flaws
which, even with my help,
were there
(obvious but understood)
because his heart was in the work
that he had done
(which my heart took);
he'd given me
the very best he could.

* * *

Lord—
here is my son.

The hills were hunkered down in mist...

The hills were hunkered down in mist,
grizzled against the wetting sky;
I felt the earth's cold loneliness—
I saw her cry,
splattering my windows with her tears;
each little hollow held a cloud,
each had its share of separate grief,
each—its shroud.

Do You not care, Lord?
do You not see?
"What is that to thee?"
He said,
"Follow thou Me."*

They met
as two boats meet:
one headed into the Harbor,
one for the open sea.
And we wonder
which
will follow
which?

*John 21:22

Don't crowd me.
I need room to grow,
to stretch my wings,
breathe deep and slow;
to look about,
to think things through;
don't hem me in,
don't block the view.

Don't push me;
I need time to grow,
to savor life from day
to day; freedom to go
at my own pace;
leisure to live more thoroughly,
unherded and unhurried, please;
just let me BE.

Don't stalk me.
Follow where *He* leads
though it may mean
another path, one needs
one single aim in life:
follow well, work hard,
obedient and faithful. So
Go!—after God.

My world is blanketed today
in silent white
that fell without a sound
all through the night.
It padded every crooked rail,
it carpeted the lawn,
transfiguring each naked twig;
and with the dawn
I smiled to see,
upholstered and serene,
the children's swing
beneath the tree,
incongruous in this wintry scene
. . . awaiting Spring.

Atop the ridge...

Atop the ridge,
against the sky
where clouds,
windwhipped,
sail free, sail high;
a tree uprooted,
fell and lodged
in the forks of an oak tree
standing by.

There they stood—
felled,
upheld,
in the windswept wood.

Atop the ridge
I found them there
one cold Spring day;
and stopped
to stare;

and stayed
to pray.

It reminded me how Daddy held up Mother after her stroke.

O tenderest Love,
how we do fail
through our own folly
to avail
ourselves of You.
Cold,
we shun
Your warmth,
Your sun;
dry,
Your dew,
Your everflowing Spring;
and pressured much,
we miss Your gentle,
calming touch;
then wonder, "Why?"
O pitying Heart,
forgive
the pauper spirit
that would live
a beggar
at Your Open Gate
until it is too late
—too late.

It is no nightingale
tonight,
no whippoorwill,
enchanting pale
twilight
with singing
on the hill
for us . . .
only the limpid frogs,
hatched in the damp
someplace,
raising their hallelujah
chorus
loud:
. . . and I am touched
with grace.

To heal a hate
takes grace
that isn't. There
is churning hurt
and bitterness
—and black despair.
No love. No grace.
No power to choose.

I heard a stillness.
Then
I felt His face.
His searching eyes
held mine
and would not turn me loose.
Then through hot tears
I saw and understood:
He hung cross high,
a spear was in my hand
that dripped with blood,
a helmet on my head.
I watched Him die;
but just before, He said,
"Forgive them for
they know not what
they do" . . .*
then He was dead.

Slowly I raised my head:
the clouds were unarranged,
the sky was fair,
the warm sun shone,
nothing had changed:
the hurt still there
only . . .
the hate was gone.

*Luke 23:34

158

I think it harder
Lord, to cast
the cares of those I love
on You,
than to cast mine.
We, growing older,
learn at last
that You
are merciful
and kind.
Not one time
have You failed me,
Lord—
why fear that you'll
fail mine?

God, look who my daddy is!

God,
look who my Daddy is!
He is the one
who wore his guardian angel out
(he thought it fun).
First, it was bikes:
he tore around those hills
like something wild,
breaking his bones
in one of many spills;
next, it was cars:
how fast he drove (though well)
only patrolmen
and his guardian angel knew;
the first complained,
the second never tells.
Then it was planes:
that was the closest we
ever got—till now.
I never knew him well
except that he
kept that angelic guardian
on his toes.

Not long ago
You touched him,
and he turned.
Oh, Lord, what grace!
(and how quizzical the look
upon his angel's face:
a sort of skidding-to-a-stop
to change his pace.)

And now, he just had me:
which only shows
who needs a little angel of his own
to keep *him* on *his* toes.
Oh, humorous vengeance!
Recompense—with fun!
I'll keep *him* busy, Lord.
Well done! Well done!

Like Pharisees
do we condemn
before both man and God,
one who slipped
and whose clothing
is smeared with sod;

Could we but hear
His voice,
stern above our own,
"Let him without sin
among you,
first cast a stone!"*

I met you years ago
when
of all the men
I knew,
you,
I hero-worshiped
then:
you are my husband now . . .
my husband!
and from my home
(your arms),
I turn to look
down the long trail of years
to where I met you first
and hero-worshiped,
and I would smile;
. . . I know you better now:
the faults,
the odd preferments,
the differences
that make you *you*.
That other me
—so young,
so far away—
saw you
and hero-worshiped
but never *knew*;
while I,
grown wiser
with the closeness of these years,
hero-worship, too!

Puppet,
poor puppet,
who's pulling your strings?

Puppets can't answer,
puppets just swing;
puppets just hang there
docile and sweet,
kill on command
and riot in the street.

Puppet,
poor puppet,
who's pulling your strings?

When
in the morning
I make our bed,
pulling his sheets
and covers tight,
I know the tears
I shouldn't shed
will fall unbidden
as the rain;
and I would kneel,
praying again
words I mean
but cannot feel.

"Lord,
not my will
but Thine
be done."
The doubts dissolving
one by one . . .

For I will realize
as I pray,
that's why it happened
. . . and this way.

Where does one turn
at such a time
as this?
Where find concern
that once was mine,
such bliss
as a loved child
knows within his home
when small?
The whole world smiled
and that loved home
was all.

Where does one turn
at such a time
as this?
Lord, but to You
Whose gentle "Come"
is
assurance strong of love
of warmth and safety, too,
of bliss—
and I am Home.

...done with play ...

"I'm Daniel Creasman's mother.
I brung these clothes
so's you
could dress him up real natural-like—
no . . .
navy wouldn't do.
He liked this little playsuit—
it's sorta faded now—
that tore place he
he got tryin'
to help his daddy plow.
No . . .
if he dressed real smart-like—
and all that fancy trim—
the last we'd see of Danny,
it wouldn't seem
like him.
But . . .
comb his hair . . . real special . . .
(if 'twouldn't seem
too odd) . . .
I brush it so
come Sunday
when he goes
to the house of God."

That afternoon
I saw him—
so still, so tanned he lay—
with the faded blue suit on him,
like he'd just come in from play . . .
but his hair was brushed
"real special" . . .
and it didn't seem
one bit odd,
for . . .
he was just a small boy,
done with play
gone home to the house of God.

Tonight
I have a roof of slate
to look upon.
Cool rain,
like Scottish mist,
falls gently and
the sun is gone
—setting late—
and I am still,
listening to
the reassuring of a dove
upon the sill;
a long day's journey
ending thus
in tired ease,
above a cobbled courtyard
grayed with age,
wrapped in peace . . .

Armathwaite Hall, England

Oh, time! be slow!
it was a dawn ago
I was a child
dreaming of being grown;
a noon ago
I was
with children of my own;
and now
it's afternoon
—and late—
and they are grown
and gone.
Time, wait!

Beyond those hills
lie yesterday,
the silenced now,
and a tomorrow.
The clouds
that wrap those hills
like shrouds
are free to come and go
at will:
no guns can frighten
them away
nor stop the moon
and stars, nor say
the sun must shine.
No manifesto tells the rain
where it must fall,
how much
and when.

The very air
they breathe
(on which their life depends)
comes from the One
Whom they deny.
And yet He sends
them rain and sun
and air to breathe.

And here and there
does one look up
and see,
and know
He is,
and He is There?

Hong Kong, 1973, looking across the border to mainland
China.

I need Your help
in the evening
more, I think,
than at dawn.
For tiredness comes
with twilight,
and my resolves
are gone.
I'm thinking of rest
not service,
of valleys
instead of steeps,
and my dreams are not
of conquest
but the blissful oblivion
of sleep.

We are told
to wait on You.
But, Lord,
there is no time.
My heart implores
upon its knees,
"Hurry!
. . . please."

... a last bright leaf ...

I love these last details of Fall
when past its prime;
the graying hills,
no longer color-crowded, climb,
subdued, to meet a brilliant sky;
when sunlight spills,
filtering through branches
newly bare,
to warm
a newly covered ground,
and light the way
for tired leaves
still falling down.

To see a spray of yellow leaves
illumining wet,
rain-blackened trees,
stabs with a joy
akin to pain
that pauses
but to stab again:
when round the corner,
like a shout,
a single, crimson
tree stands out!

After the whole
is bedded down
upon the earth's vast
compost heap,
and sight gives place
to faith and hope,
walking up the mountain slope,
lying on my path I find
a last bright leaf
for me to keep.

Train our love
that it may grow
slowly . . . deeply . . . steadily;
till our hearts will overflow
unrestrained and readily.

Discipline it, too,
dear God;
strength of steel
throughout the whole.
Teach us patience,
thoughtfulness,
tenderness, and
self-control.

Deepen it
throughout the years,
age and mellow it
until,
time that finds us
old without,
within,
will find us
lovers still.

It was a lonely
desperate search
that led her up one street and down
another, looking for a church
where she could kneel and pray.
She looked Prague through
that somber day—
(what was left of a woman's heart,
God knew).
Yet each was boarded up
(where does one take despair?),
on each a notice nailed:
"closed . . . for repair."*

                    * * *

Year followed year:
wars . . .
elections . . .
death . . .
each country wrapped
within its own affairs.
The evening news
kept all aware
of Vietnam,
Ireland,
the Middle East,
and Chad.
Few ever thought of God's house
"closed . . . for repair,"
and if they had
nothing was said,
presuming it dead.

Till one day came
a writer without fear,‡
and those with time to read
took time to hear.
That which we thought was dead,
of which we all despaired,
showed signs of reemerging:

. . . repaired!

*From Marcia Davenport's *Too Strong for Fantasy*.
‡Alexander Solzhenitsyn
1975

God,
it grows darker
day by day;
blood stains the present
and the future may
well be history's dark night.
Deliverance (at times)
and yet death might
best serve Your ends.
You choose, not they
who do the deed.
They plot, You laugh.*
You knew
when they had killed
before,
they did what You
had willed:
no less—
no more.

Lord, I am filled
with wonder
(who had been filled
with fears),
for
I hear Your laughter
when I hear the thunder,
and when I feel the raindrops,
feel Your tears.

*Psalm 2:4

How can I pray
while my heart cries,
"You killed
my son"?
What can I say?
How look for comfort
from the One
Who willed
it done?
Omnipotent, He could
have stopped it
if He would;
my son . . . my son . . .
numb with grief,
my soul is one vast "why?"
his life was all too brief;
he was so young
to die.
Where were You,
Lord?
Where were You?

Gently He replied,
"Just where I was,
dearly, dearly loved,
when Mine
was crucified."

And when I die
I hope my soul ascends
slowly, so that I
may watch the earth receding
out of sight,
its vastness growing smaller
as I rise,
savoring its recession
with delight.
Anticipating joy
is itself a joy.
And joy unspeakable
and full of glory
needs more
than "in the twinkling of an eye,"*
more than "in a moment."
Lord, who am I
to disagree?
It's only we
have much
to leave behind;
so much . . . Before.
These moments
of transition
will, for me, be
time
to adore.

*1 Corinthians 15:52

...there'll be spring!

Show me a small
and shriveled seed,
discarded
as a worthless thing:
smile
if you will,
that I should kneel
in worship
—there'll be Spring!

Titles, start caps and divider copy hand styled in Brazos,
a contemporary, light letter form of beautiful simplicity
designed exclusively for Word, Inc.

Text set in Palatino, a graceful twentieth-century typeface
designed by Hermann Zapf of West Germany.

The designer gratefully acknowledges the help of
Dennis Hill, Mary Ruth Howes and Carol Kilpatrick
in the design and production of this book.

Typography by Peri-graphics, Waco, Texas.

Designed by Ronald E. Garman.